Trombones or Euphoniums TC

Starter Duets

Philip Sparke

© 2007 by **Anglo Music Press**
PO Box 303, Wembley, HA9 8GX, England
Copyright secured / All rights reserved

STARTER DUETS
Trombones or Euphoniums TC
Philip Sparke

Order Number: AMP 222-401
ISMN: M 57029 221 9

Printed in the EU

Contents

	Page		Page
About this edition	4		
1. Jeepers Creepers	5	31. Wicked Waltz	18
2. Two Together	5	32. Follow Me	19
3. One More Time	5	33. Spanish Scherzo	19
4. Up and Down the Stairs	5	34. Czardas	20
5. Three-legged Race	6	35. Peter's Polka	20
6. Once More	6	36. Pierrot's Puppet	21
7. Upside Down	6	37. Highland Tune	21
8. Heroes' March	7	38. Bluebird's Ballad	22
9. Peasants' Dance	7	39. Simple Serenade	22
10. Give Us a Break	8	40. Dance of the Dolls	23
11. The Bits In-between	8	41. Bobby Who?	23
12. Wednesday Waltz	9	42. Scottish Air	24
13. A Little Fanfare	9	43. Spooks	24
14. Another Little Fanfare	10	44. Sad March	25
15. A Tune without a Name	10	45. Willow Waltz	25
16. Step by Step	11	46. Canzona	26
17. Purple Patch	11	47. Love Song	26
18. Scottish Gavottish	12	48. Dynamic Exercise	27
19. The Village Band	12	49. The Blue Danube	28
20. In the Country	13	50. All's Well	28
21. In the Air	13	51. Alpenhorn Echoes	29
22. The Traveller	14	52. Sunday Scherzo	30
23. Do You Agree?	14	53. Carol	30
24. Westminster Waltz	15	54. Going Home Again	31
25. Rushing Around	15	55. Trumpet Tune	32
26. Bobby's Blues	16	56. Music Box Waltz	32
27. Beach Cruise	16	57. Ragtime	33
28. Sparrow's Dance	17	58. Men of Harlech	34
29. Number Twenty-nine	17	59. Footsteps	35
30. Harvest Time	18	60. Rock School	36
		Über diese Ausgabe	37
		À propos de cette édition	38
		Over deze uitgave	39

About this edition

The early stages of learning any instrument are undoubtedly the most important. A good teacher is of course essential but it is also vital to have stimulating pieces to play, which complement your choice of teaching method, and are carefully tailored to introduce learning and playing skills in a structured manner.

As in my book of *Starter Studies*, the duets in this book introduce new musical elements in a logical order to facilitate the speedy growth of the 'complete musician', with the obvious benefit of allowing teacher and student (or two students) to play together and therefore experience the benefits of ensemble playing early in the learning process.

So, may I wish you lots of fun with these duets as you start out in the great world of music!

Enjoy!

Philip Sparke

Philip Sparke was born in London in 1951 and studied composition, trumpet and piano at the Royal College of Music, where he gained an ARCM.

It was at the College that his interest in writing instrumental music arose, alongside his compositions for concert band and brass band. He studied trumpet with Bob Walton who encouraged him to write his own studies for the instrument, as well as brass and wind chamber music for various student performing groups.

His solo pieces for brass and woodwind instruments have appeared in the syllabuses of all the various UK examination boards and this led him to compiling scale books and being commissioned to write sight-reading exercises and recital pieces for the major syllabuses in the UK.

He regularly adjudicates at music festivals around the UK and has travelled to most European countries, Australia, New Zealand, Japan and the USA.

He runs his own publishing company, *Anglo Music Press,* which he formed in May 2000. In September 2000 he was awarded the Iles Medal of the Worshipful Company of Musicians for his services to brass bands.

Starter Duets

60 Progressive Duets for Trombones or Euphoniums TC

Philip Sparke

1. Jeepers Creepers

2. Two Together

3. One More Time

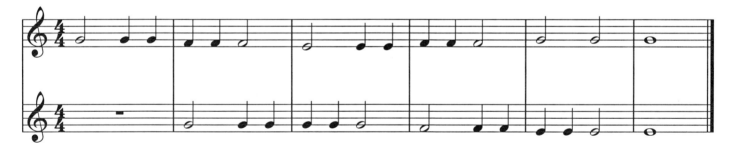

4. Up and Down the Stairs

5. Three-legged Race

6. Once More

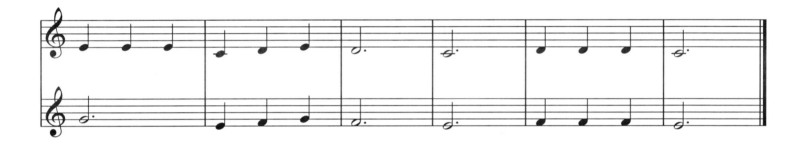

7. Upside Down

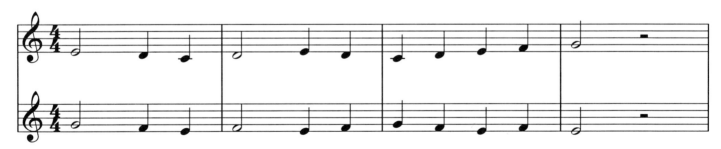

8. Heroes' March

9. Peasants' Dance

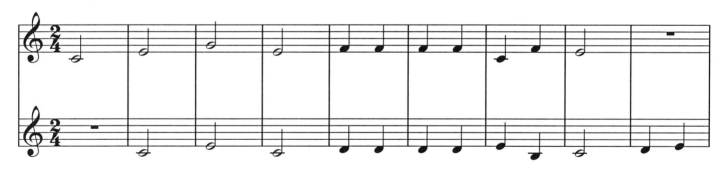

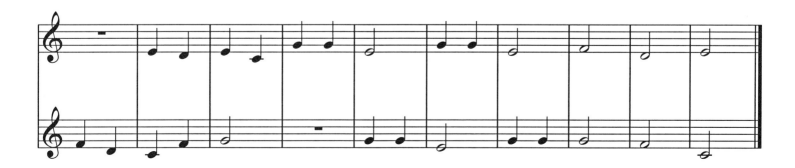

10. Give Us a Break

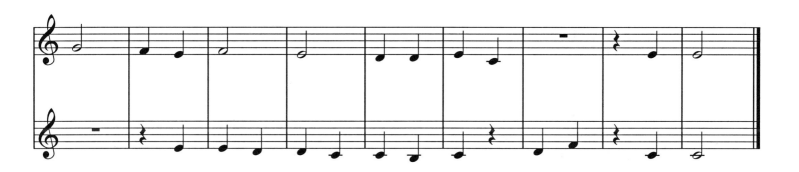

11. The Bits In-between

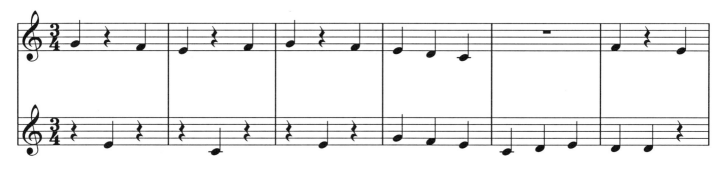

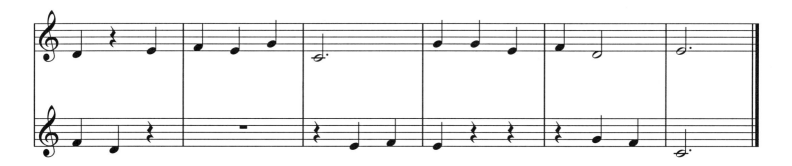

12. Wednesday Waltz

13. A Little Fanfare

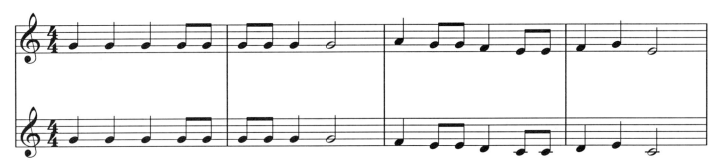

14. Another Little Fanfare

15. A Tune without a Name

16. Step by Step

17. Purple Patch

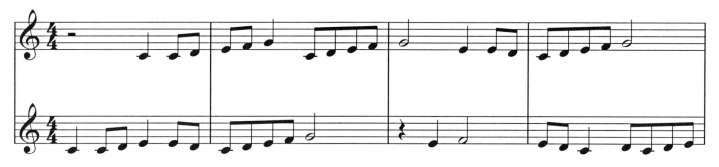

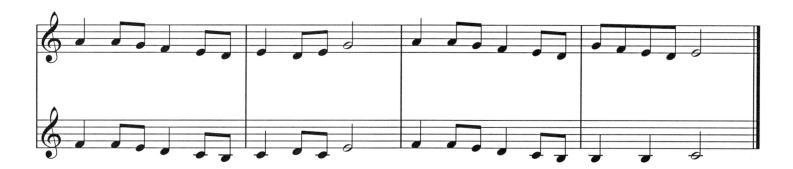

18. Scottish Gavottish

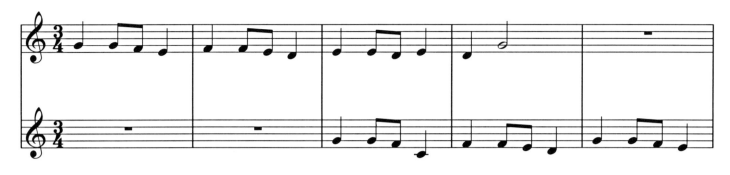

19. The Village Band

20. In the Country

21. In the Air

22. The Traveller

23. Do You Agree?

24. Westminster Waltz

25. Rushing Around

26. Bobby's Blues

27. Beach Cruise

28. Sparrow's Dance

29. Number Twenty-nine

30. Harvest Time

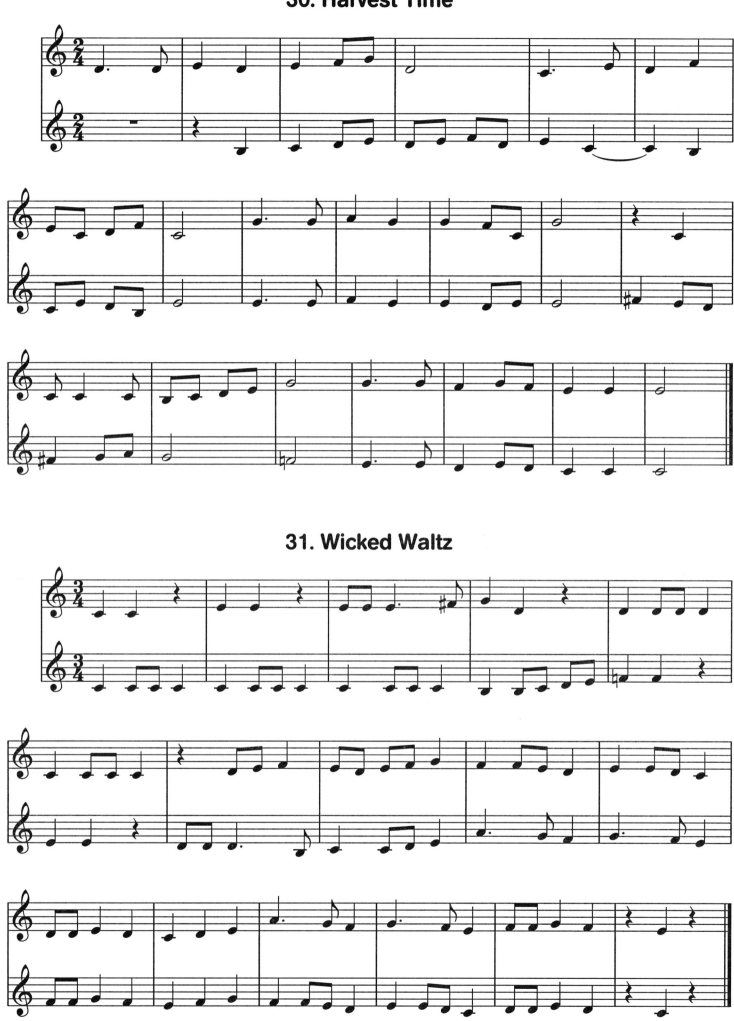

31. Wicked Waltz

32. Follow Me

33. Spanish Scherzo

34. Czardas

35. Peter's Polka

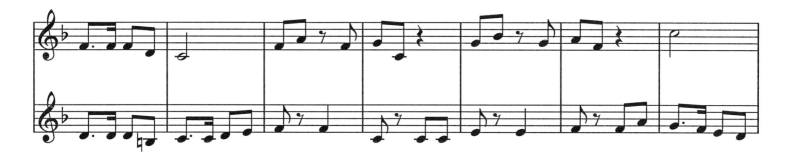

36. Pierrot's Puppet

37. Highland Tune

38. Bluebird's Ballad

39. Simple Serenade

40. Dance of the Dolls

41. Bobby Who?

42. Scottish Air

43. Spooks

24

44. Sad March

45. Willow Waltz

46. Canzona

47. Love Song

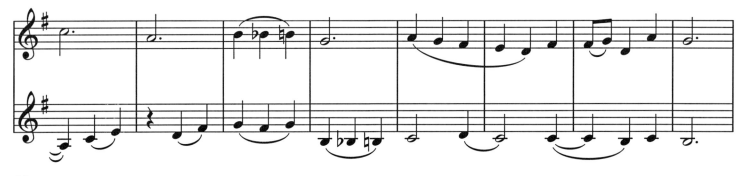

26

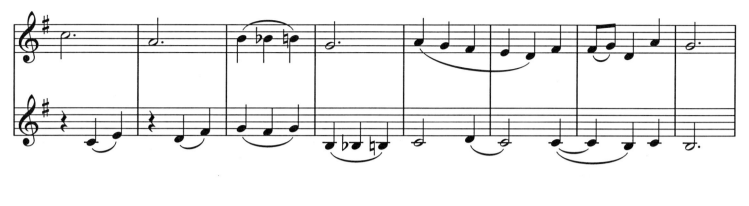

48. Dynamic Exercise

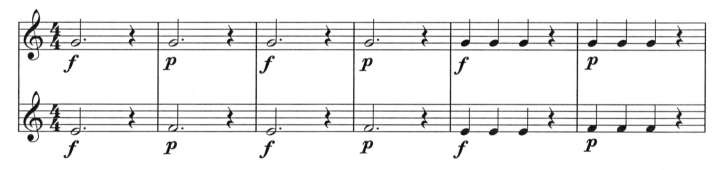

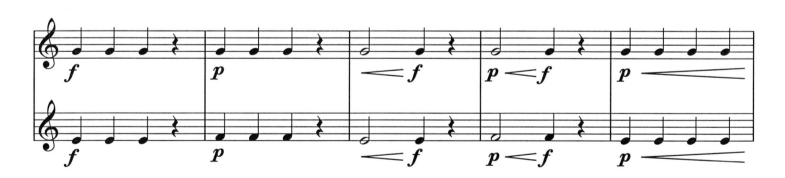

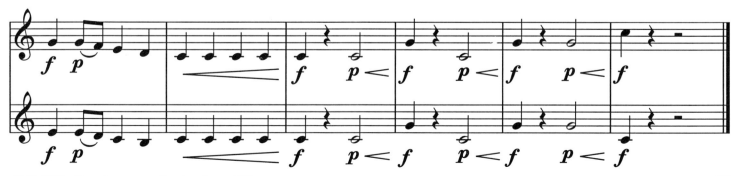

49. The Blue Danube

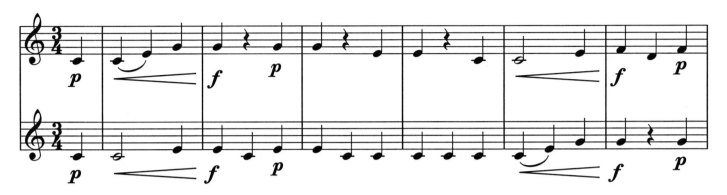

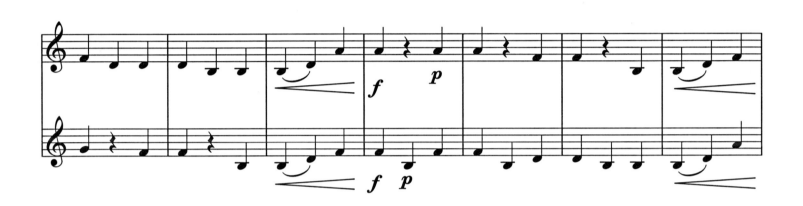

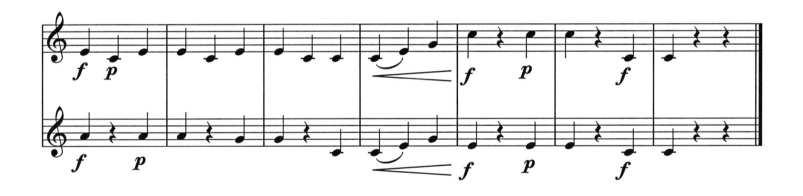

50. All's Well

51. Alpenhorn Echoes

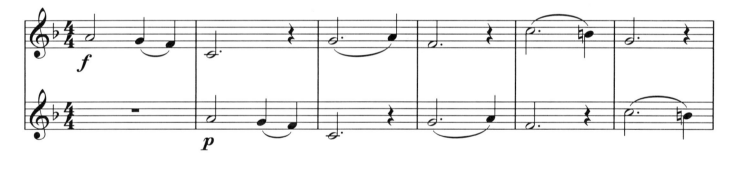

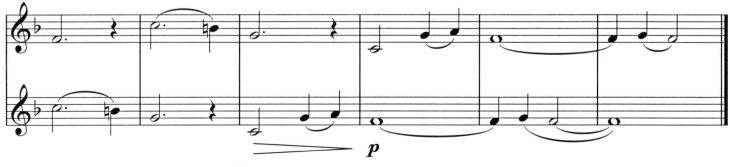

52. Sunday Scherzo

53. Carol

30

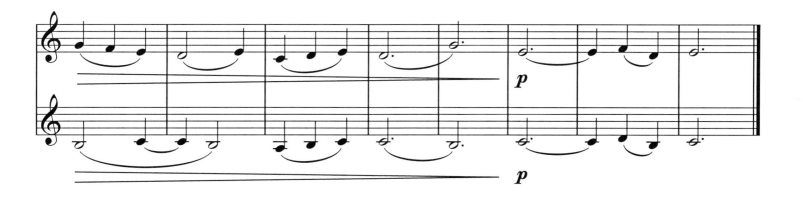

54. Going Home Again

55. Trumpet Tune

56. Music Box Waltz

57. Ragtime

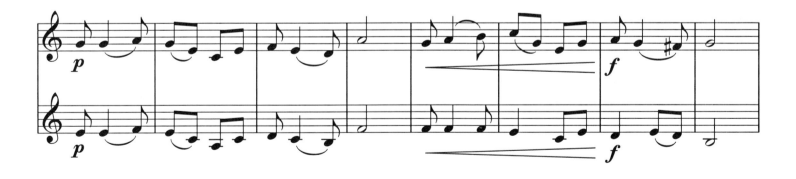

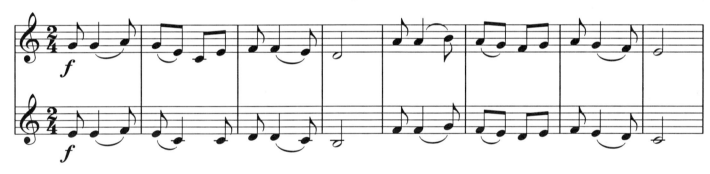

58. Men of Harlech

59. Footsteps

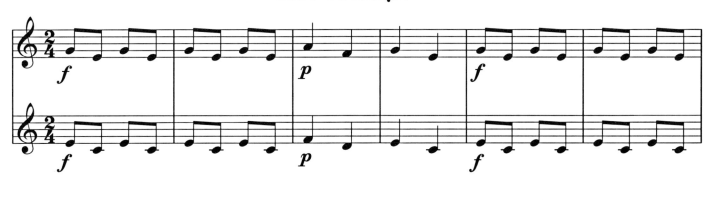

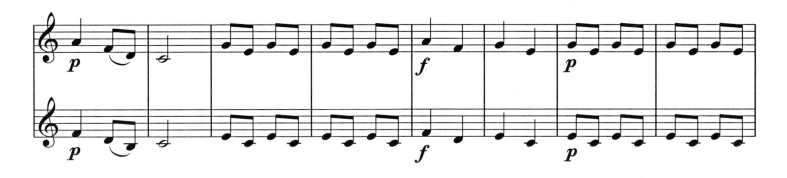

60. Rock School

Über diese Ausgabe

Das frühe Lernstadium ist im Unterricht für jedes Instrument zweifellos das Wichtigste. Ein guter Lehrer ist natürlich ebenfalls unentbehrlich. Von großer Bedeutung ist aber auch, motivierendes Lehrmaterial zur Verfügung zu haben, das die gewählte Lehrmethode ergänzt und sorgfältig auf eine strukturierte Einführung von Theorie und Spielfertigkeiten zugeschnitten ist.

Wie auch meine bereits erschienenen STARTER STUDIES, führen die Duette in diesem Buch neue musikalische Elemente in einer logischen Reihenfolge ein, um die rasche Entwicklung der Schüler zu „ausgereiften Musikern" zu fördern, verbunden mit dem klaren Nutzen, der in der Möglichkeit des Zusammenspiels von Lehrer und Schüler (oder von zwei Schülern) liegt. So werden schon im frühen Lernstadium wertvolle Erfahrungen im Ensemblespiel gesammelt.

Nun darf ich allen, die in die große Welt der Musik aufbrechen, viel Spaß mit diesen Duetten wünschen!

Viel Vergnügen!

Philip Sparke

Philip Sparke wurde 1951 in London geboren. Er studierte Komposition, Trompete und Klavier am Royal College of Music und wurde dort als ARCM (Associate of the Royal College of Music) ausgezeichnet.

Zu dieser Zeit erwachte sein Interesse, parallel zu Kompositionen für Blasorchester und Brass Bands, auch Instrumentalmusik zu schreiben. Er studierte Trompete bei Bob Walton, der ihn ermutigte, eigene Etüden für dieses Instrument und Kammermusik für Bläser und Blechbläser für verschiedene Studentenensembles zu schreiben.

Philip Sparkes Solostücke für Blech- und Holzbläser wurden in die Lehrpläne aller unterschiedlichen Prüfungsausschüsse Großbritanniens aufgenommen. Dies führte dazu, dass er Skalenbücher zusammenstellte und beauftragt wurde, Vom Blatt-Leseübungen und Konzertstücke für die wichtigsten Lehrpläne Großbritanniens zu schreiben.

Regelmäßig ist er als Berater bei Musikfestivals in Großbritannien tätig. Seine Reisen führten ihn in die meisten europäischen Länder, nach Australien, Neuseeland, Japan und in die USA.

Philip Sparke leitet einen eigenen Musikverlag, *Anglo Music Press*, gegründet im Mai 2000. Im September 2000 erhielt er die Iles Medal of the Worshipful Company of Music für seine Verdienste um den Brass Band-Bereich.

À propos de cette édition

Les débuts de l'apprentissage d'un instrument sont certainement les plus décisifs. Un bon professeur est un élément-clé, mais il est indispensable de posséder, en complément de la méthode utilisée, des outils pédagogiques motivants offrant une présentation structurée des techniques de jeu et d'apprentissage.

À l'instar des études publiées dans le recueil *Starter Studies*, ces duos introduisent de nouveaux éléments musicaux en suivant une démarche logique qui facilite le développement rapide d'un "musicien complet". Le fait de pouvoir jouer avec son professeur (ou un autre élève) permet à l'instrumentiste débutant de découvrir la richesse et l'importance du jeu en ensemble et ce très tôt dans l'apprentissage.

Que ces duos constituent les premiers pas plaisants de votre entrée dans le formidable monde de la musique !

Amusez-vous bien !

Philip Sparke

Né en 1951 à Londres, Philip Sparke étudie la composition, la trompette et le piano au prestigieux Collège Royal de Musique de Londres où il obtient l'Associate Diploma (ARCM).

Il se découvre un intérêt pour la composition de musique instrumentale et d'œuvres pour Orchestre d'Harmonie et Brass Band alors qu'il fréquente le Collège Royal. Sous l'impulsion de son professeur de trompette, Bob Walton, Philip Sparke compose des études pour trompette et des pièces de musique de chambre pour instruments à vent (bois / cuivres) destinés à divers ensembles instrumentaux estudiantins.

Ses pièces solos pour cuivres et bois figurent au répertoire des œuvres de concours et d'examens nationaux du Royaume-Uni. Il rédigera par la suite plusieurs recueils de gammes. De nombreuses commandes de pièces de récital et d'exercices de lecture à vue lui parviennent alors, notamment du comité chargé des principaux programmes éducatifs nationaux.

Philip Sparke est un membre de jury très sollicité lors de concours et d'événements nationaux ou dans la plupart des pays d'Europe, en Australie, en Nouvelle-Zélande, au Japon et aux États-Unis.

Depuis mai 2000, il publie ses compositions sous son label *Anglo Music Press*. En septembre 2000, l'association britannique Worshipful Company of Musicians le récompense de la prestigieuse Iles Medal pour son engagement en faveur des Brass Bands.

Over deze uitgave

De vroege stadia van het leren bespelen van een instrument zijn ongetwijfeld de voornaamste. Een goede docent is natuurlijk essentieel, maar het is eveneens van groot belang om motiverende stukken te spelen, die bovendien de keuze voor een leermethode aanvullen en structuur bieden bij de introductie van leer- en speelvaardigheden.

Net als de stukken in mijn eerdere uitgave *Starter Studies* introduceren de duetten in dit boek nieuwe muzikale elementen in een logische volgorde – om de ontwikkeling van de complete muzikant te bevorderen. Uiteraard bieden duetten een extra voordeel: docent en leerling (of twee leerlingen) kunnen samen musiceren, zodat de leerling al vroeg in het leerproces ervaart hoe leerzaam en leuk samenspel kan zijn.

Rest mij nog eenieder veel plezier te wensen met deze duetten – en bij de entree in de fantastische wereld van de muziek.

Veel speelgenoegen!

Philip Sparke

Philip Sparke werd in 1951 in Londen geboren en studeerde compositie, trompet en piano aan het Royal College of Music, waar hij het ARCM-diploma haalde (Associate of the Royal College of Music).

Tijdens deze opleiding groeide zijn belangstelling voor het schrijven van instrumentale muziek, naast zijn composities voor harmonieorkest en brassband. Hij studeerde trompet bij Bob Walton, die hem aanmoedigde om zijn eigen etudes voor dit instrument te schrijven, evenals muziek voor brassband en blaasensemble voor diverse studentengroepen.

Zijn solostukken voor koper- en houtinstrumenten zijn verschenen in de leerplannen van alle verschillende examencommissies van Groot-Brittannië; dit bracht hem ertoe om boeken met toonladderstudies samen te stellen. Bovendien schreef hij in opdracht oefeningen voor het spelen van blad en speelstukken voor de belangrijkste leerplannen in Groot-Brittannië.

Philip Sparke zit regelmatig in jury's van muziekfestivals in Groot-Brittannië en zijn dirigeer- en juryactiviteiten brachten hem naar de meeste Europese landen, Australië, Nieuw-Zeeland, Japan en de Verenigde Staten.

Hij publiceert zijn eigen werken onder zijn eigen label, *Anglo Music Press*, opgericht in mei 2000. In september 2000 ontving hij de Iles Medal of the Worshipful Company of Musicians voor zijn bewezen diensten aan brassbands.